Clumsy and Learning

Lotus Blossom

BookLeaf Publishing
India | USA | UK

Presentation by *BookLeaf Publishing*

Web: www.bookleafpub.com

E-mail: info@bookleafpub.com

ISBN: 9789357444767

First edition 2022

DEDICATION

This book is dedicated to all my fellow first-year university students who need a bit of a laugh.

ACKNOWLEDGEMENT

Thanks to my dear friend Caitlyn who roped me into this adventure.

Keeping Myself Sane

A whirlwind of ramshackle fun,
A poem for everyone,
They're short and sweet,
A uni treat,
Made to get me through year one.

My Work Ethic

I have an assignment that's due,
Or I could watch The Office, wouldn't you?
Oh, just one more,
Now it's quarter to four,
My assignment is late, I am screwed.

All I Do is Eat Toast and Talk to My Cat

I can't be f**ked getting dressed,
I'm grumpy and constantly stressed,
No thoughts in my head,
I'll just stay in bed,
So cheers, to being depressed.

8am Zoom Lectures

My eyes are crusty with sleep,
I can barely stand on my feet,
I'm in my pajamas,
Slept through my alarms,
I've had no coffee. I weep.

The 5pm Shakes

Now the house is clean and vacuumed,
There's candles lit round the room.
My plants are fed,
I've made the bed,
Oh god, that caffeine's making me zoom.

Red P Plates and Freedom

I love my little match-box car,
her paint is peeling but we've gone far,
speed to the coast,
we'll make the most,
of youth, a fire, and my guitar.

Monday Hangovers

Wrapped up in my doona cocoon,
I wish again for stars and moon,
I need to pee,
And I can't see,
I'll maybe think about getting up soon.

The Dog Ate That Pav

I creep up the stairs on tiptoe,
And open the fridge door real slow.
What'll I have?
Some cheese or that pav?
Don't worry, mum will never know.

Apology To My Lecturers

My lectures on zoom and I'm stuck,
On Reddit just laughing at ducks,
In walks my mum,
I say something dumb,
My mic's been unmuted, oh f**k.

Couch Potato Days

I love the days when nothing's on,
When the sun's out and the clouds are gone,
Nothing to do,
The sky is blue,
I'll be on the couch just snoozing on.

Ultimate Satisfaction

As many tabs open as are under the sun,
My assignment is finally over and done.
The tabs are lined up,
With that X at the top,
Now I can close them all one by one.

Happiness in My Favorite Mug

These days I live off tea
(Black, herbal, or green).
A dash of milk,
Smooth as silk,
No sugar, a drop of honey.

Crook as a Chook

I wanna be at the gym, but no,
I'm crook and have to stay at home,
I wanna pump iron,
But I would be lying',
If I said I was okay to go.

Benzodiazepines

Two exams done and I can only try,
To keep up my study and try not to cry.
I'm so stressed out,
I've got no doubt,
That soon I'll just be asking "why…?"

Pick Your Poison

There's nothing else that quite compares,
When your feet are kicked up with no worries or cares,
When the day is done,
And the TV's on,
And you can enjoy some nice cold beers.

On My Way to Being in Debt

I must confess, I cannot lie,
There're many things I'd love to buy.
A brand new hat,
Or a cute toy bat,
Even though my income's dry.

Call Me Innocent

I don't always know what to do with my life,
I just hope I don't run into very much strife.
I just wanna party,
Be a lil' bit naughty,
I wanna stay young, and I think that's alright.

Til' Next Year

Thank you for reading I hope you had fun,
I hope you can share it with everyone.
Now go grab a beer,
And some holiday cheer,
For exams and year one, they are finally done.

www.ingramcontent.com/pod-product-compliance
Lightning Source LLC
Chambersburg PA
CBHW051721130826
49812CB00034B/1286
* 9 7 8 9 3 5 7 4 4 4 7 6 7 *